GET ACTIVE!

BUILDING TEAMWORK

Written by Valerie Harvey

KidHaven PUBLISHING

Published in 2027 by
KidHaven Publishing, an Imprint of Greenhaven Publishing, LLC
2544 Clinton St., Buffalo, NY 14224

Written by: Valerie Harvey
Edited by: Elise Carraway
Designed by: Jasmine Pointer

All facts, statistics, web addresses, and URLs in this book were verified as valid and accurate at time of writing. No responsibility for any changes to external websites or references can be accepted by either the author or publisher.

Cataloging-in-Publication Data

Names: Harvey, Valerie.
Title: Building teamwork / Valerie Harvey.
Description: Buffalo, NY : KidHaven Publishing, 2027. | Series: Get active! | Includes glossary and index.
Identifiers: ISBN 9781534570825 (pbk.) | ISBN 9781534570832 (library bound) | ISBN 9781534570849 (ebook)
Subjects: LCSH: Teamwork (Sports)--Juvenile literature. | Sportsmanship--Juvenile literature.
Classification: LCC GV706.8 H378 2027 | DDC 796--dc23

Printed in China

CPSIA compliance information: Batch #QS27KH: For further information contact Greenhaven Publishing LLC at 1-844-317-7404.

Please visit our website, www.greenhavenpublishing.com. For a free color catalog of all our high-quality books, call toll free 1-844-317-7404 or fax 1-844-317-7405.

Find us on

Image Credits. All images are courtesy of Shutterstock.com, unless otherwise stated.

Recurring – Tatiana Kubara, VVadi4ka. Cover – PeopleImages. 2–3 – PeopleImages. 4–5 – Maxim Studio, New Africa. 6–7 – Rawpixel.com, Fotokostic. 8–9 – Fotokostic, Olena Yakobchuk. 10–11 – Paolo Bona, Drazen Zigic. 12–13 – Media_Photos, Zamrznuti tonovi. 14–15 – Click Images, JoeSAPhotos. 16–17 – Sergey Novikov, Gorynvd. 18–19 – Suzanne Tucker, PeopleImages. 20–21 – Corepics VOF, Barbara Kalbfleisch. 22–23 – Jacob Lund, PeopleImages.

CONTENTS

Words that look like <u>this</u> can be found in the glossary on page 24.

WELCOME TO GET ACTIVE!

Are you ready to get active? Being an active person means getting your body moving. You can take part in all sorts of games, sports, and activities as part of being active.

Getting active is a great chance to build teamwork. Many sports and games you could take part in involve working with a team. Learning how to work in a team is an important skill to have.

WHAT IS TEAMWORK?

Teamwork means working with others to reach a goal. In sports, it is about helping your teammates, sharing, and listening. Everyone has a special job to do within the team.

Some sports need big teams. Others might only need a few players.

When everyone works together and supports each other, the whole team does well. Teamwork makes playing more fun, helps you make friends, and teaches you how to win and lose together with kindness and respect.

COMPETITIONS

If you take part in a team sport, you will <u>compete</u> against another team. Both teams want to win. You and your teammates must work together to try to be better than the other team.

Sometimes your team wins, and sometimes your team loses. The result is not the most important part of playing sports. The most important part is working as a team and having fun doing it.

RULES AND STRATEGIES

Rules help team sports be safe and fair. Following the rules is an important part of being a good team player. When everyone follows the rules, the game works better and everyone has more fun!

Referees make sure the rules are being followed.

Strategies are plans that teams make to help them win. A team's coach comes up with strategies that the players will use in the game. Strategies help teammates work together.

ATTACK!

In some team sports, attacking means trying to score points for your team. Many teams have a few players whose job is to try to score points.

Scoring points looks different in different sports.

Scoring points can be the most exciting part of a game. However, you cannot do it alone. You need to work with your teammates to score.

Teammates can help by passing the ball or blocking players on the other team.

DEFEND!

In team sports, defending means stopping the other team from scoring points. Defense is an important part of helping your team win. Defenders help take the pressure off the rest of the team.

Goalkeepers are important for defense.

One player cannot defend a whole team on their own. Different members of the team need to step in and help. Defenders are also sometimes known as defensive players, depending on the sport.

BALL SPORTS

Some sports are called ball sports, or ball games. They are played with a ball. There is usually only one ball, but the teams have many players. That means ball sports need teamwork!

Ball sports often involve moving a ball around a playing field to get it in a good position to score. Good team players pay attention to the game so they know who to pass to and when to do it.

SWIMMING TEAMS

Swimming might seem like a sport done by yourself. However, it can be a team sport when swimmers race in relays. In relay races, swimmers take turns in the water to try to be the fastest team.

Like with other sports, swimming teams work hard to encourage each other. They cheer each other on and want each other to do well. You can be a good teammate even when you are not competing.

ROWING TEAMS

Rowing is a sport where teams race in boats. They paddle the boats with oars. The team needs to row together to move the boat. This means a lot of teamwork is needed.

Members of a rowing team need to trust their teammates. Everybody needs to row in time with each other. If everyone rows at their own speed, the boat will not move as quickly or smoothly.

Rowing teams often choose one team member to tell them when to row.

TOTAL TEAMWORK

Teamwork at its best means everyone works together, helps each other, and tries their hardest. Each person has an important job. Good teammates listen, share, and cheer one another on.

When a team works well together, they can solve problems, play better, and have more fun. Win or lose, great teamwork makes everyone feel proud and happy to be part of the team!

GLOSSARY

COMPETE to take part in a contest with another person or team

ENCOURAGE to give someone the confidence to do something

RESPECT when someone is kind, listens, and treats others the way they want to be treated

TRUST to believe that someone will act correctly

INDEX